A Kids Guide to
Japan

By Moving Beyond the Page

Copyright © 2020 Epiphany Curriculum, LLC
By Moving Beyond the Page

All rights reserved. No part of this book may be reproduced in any form or by any electronic or mechanical means including information and retrieval systems without written permission of the publisher.

Published by Epiphany Curriculum, LLC
317 S. Broadway St., Linton, ND 58552

Printed in the USA

Japan

Japan is a country in eastern Asia. It is made up of many islands: four large ones and over 6,000 small ones!

Altogether, the size of the whole country is just a little smaller than the state of California.

Japan's capital is Tokyo, which is located on the largest island, Honshu.

Quick Facts

Official Language: Japanese
Major Religions: Buddhism and Shinto
Population: about 127 million people

The Japanese currency is the yen

The red circle on the Japanese flag represents the Sun.

In Japanese, "Japan" is pronounced "Nippon" and is written like this.

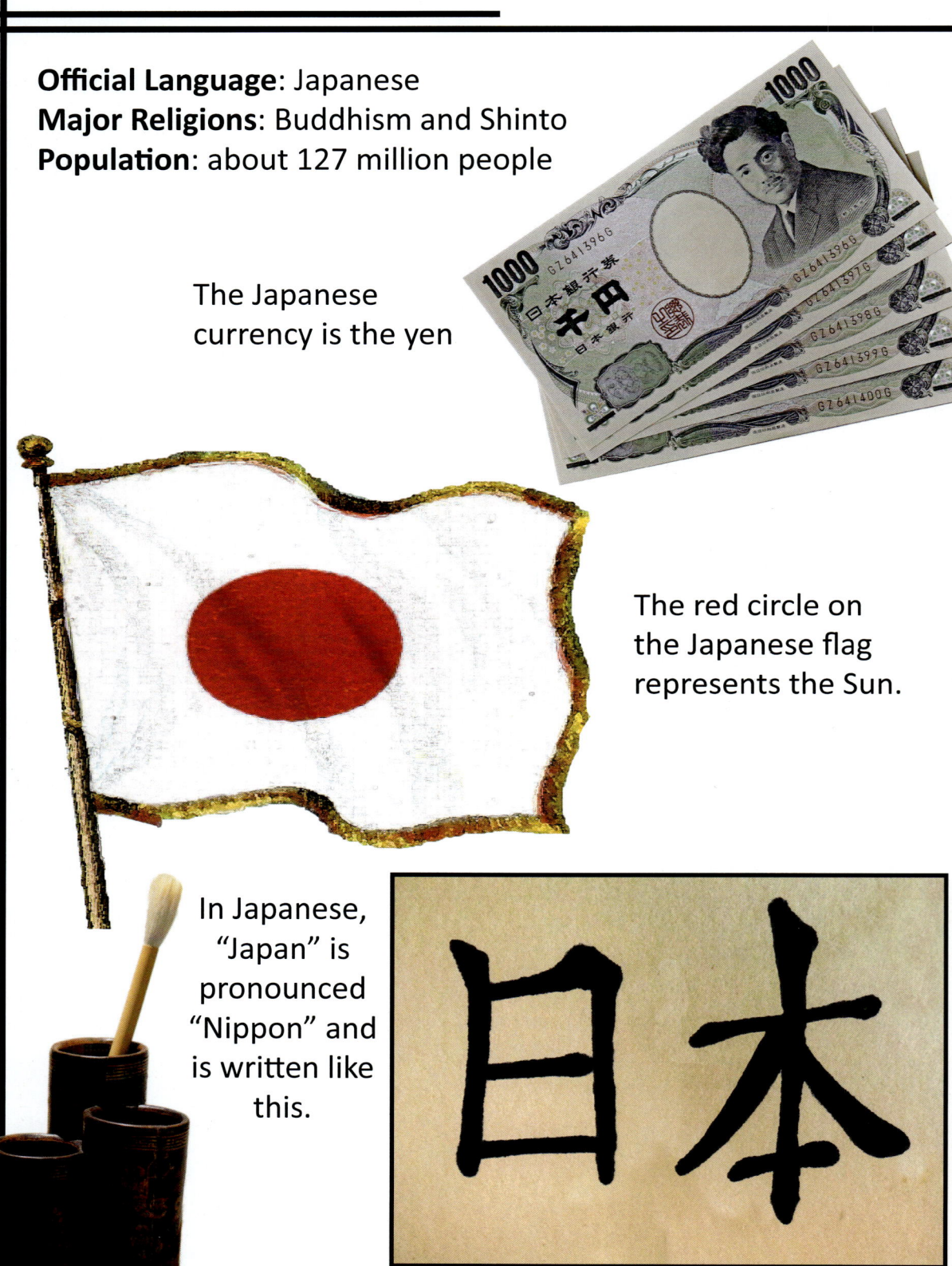

Climate and Geography

Spring in Japan is warm and dry. Visitors come from all over the world to see the cherry trees' beautiful flowers (called cherry blossoms).

Summers in Japan begin with a few weeks of very rainy days followed by a couple of months of hot and humid weather. Autumn is cool and breezy. In the winter, southern Japan is chilly but sunny while the northern areas are cold and get plenty of snow.

Japan has some beautiful forests, but about 70% of the country features mountains, including over 100 active volcanoes. The tallest point is Mount Fuji, a volcano covered in snow.

Food in Japan

Emiko is 8 years old and lives in Osaka, a large city on the island of Honshu. She sometimes has the same foods for both breakfast and dinner: rice, fish, vegetables, and miso soup (made from soy paste and fish broth). Instead of a fork, Emiko and her family use chopsticks.

Emiko helped her mother pack bento for lunch. Bento is a meal packed tightly into a box with several separate sections in it. Today Emiko has sushi (made from raw fish and rice), vegetables, and fruit.

At 3:00 in the afternoon, Emiko has a snack of onigiri (balls of rice).

Transportation

Emiko and her father ride their bicycles to the local market and to the park. To visit the art museum, they travel by subway (an underground train).

When Emiko's family travels to see her grandparents in Tokyo, they take a special train called Shinkansen, nicknamed the "bullet train" because it moves so quickly, almost 200 miles per hour!

Art

Some unique traditional art forms in Japan include ink painting on silk (a soft fabric) and calligraphy, the beautiful art of written Japanese.

Many children and adults enjoy origami, the art of folding paper to make small animals or flowers

Bonsai is the art of growing and shaping tiny trees.

Fun

Emiko likes reading manga (comic books) and watching anime (cartoons). Japanese anime, like Pokémon and Dragon Ball, is also popular in the U.S.

On weekends Emiko takes karate lessons, while her brother, Hitoshi, enjoys playing soccer.

One of Japan's most popular sports is sumo, a form of wrestling. Many people also enjoy baseball.

Traditions

Japanese history stretches back thousands of years. Many people in Japan still honor some ancient traditions.

Tea is an important part of Japanese culture. People visit teahouses to enjoy tea made in a special way and served in a traditional ceremony.

On special occasions, Japanese men and women wear traditional clothing. The kimono is a decorative robe tied around the waist with a special sash or belt called an obi.

Celebrations

Japan has many special festivals and celebrations.

The most important is Japanese New Year, celebrated the first couple of weeks of January. People clean and decorate their houses, visit family members, and eat traditional foods that are thought to bring them luck.

The Shichi-Go-San (7-5-3) Festival is held on November 15. On that day, children who are 3, girls who are 7, and boys who are 5 dress in traditional clothing, eat special candy, and visit a Shinto shrine to pray for a long and healthy life.